Hometown for an Hour

Hometown for an Hour

poems

Jennifer Rose

OHIO UNIVERSITY PRESS

ATHENS

Ohio University Press, Athens, Ohio 45701
www.ohio.edu/oupress
© 2006 by Jennifer Rose

Ohio University Press books are printed on acid-free paper ⊚ ™

14 13 12 11 10 09 08 07 06   5 4 3 2 1

Library of Congress Cataloging-in-Publication Data
Rose, Jennifer, 1959–
   Hometown for an hour : poems / Jennifer Rose.
      p. cm.
   ISBN 0-8214-1655-3 (cloth : alk. paper) — ISBN 0-8214-1656-1 (pbk. : alk. paper)
   I. Title.
   PS3568.O7632H66 2006
   811'.54—dc22

                              2005028686

Acknowledgments

Some of these poems originally appeared in *The Nation* ("Maintenon Postcard" and "Lipik Postcard"); *Ploughshares* ("Winter, Chicago"); *Agni* ("Harvard Square Postcard" and "Mostar Postcard"); *Antioch Review* ("Country Erotica"); *Shenandoah* ("The Storm"); *Verse* ("Southern Postcard" and "Gettysburg Postcard"); *Denver Quarterly* ("Route 1 Postcard"); *The Women's Review of Books* ("Off-Season" and "Cape Cod Postcard"); *Main Street News* ("Kentuckiana Postcards"); *Southern Poetry Review* ("Appomatox Postcard"); *The Journal* ("Corydon Postcard" and "Mt. San Angelo Postcard"); *Willow Review* ("Evanston Postcard"); *Margie Review* ("Country Headache" and "Country Holiday"); *Just outside the Frame: Poets from the Santa Fe Broadside* ("Delaware Park Postcard" and "Provincetown Postcard"); and in *The 1989 Grolier Poetry Prize Anthology* ("Cape Cod Postcard"). "Lipik Postcard," "Mostar Postcard," and "Letter from Orahovica" also appeared in *The Old Direction of Heaven* (Truman State University, 2000). Online credits include *The Poetry Porch* ("Lipik Postcard," "Mostar Postcard," "Southern Postcard," "Gettysburg Postcard," and "Cape Cod Postcard"); *Santa Fe Poetry Broadside* ("Evanston Postcard," "Delaware Park Postcard," and "Provincetown Postcard"); and *The Drunken Boat* ("Lake Forest Postcard" and "Metaphors at Low Tide").

Many thanks to these editors and to the National Endowment for the Arts, Massachusetts Cultural Council, Waltham Arts Lottery, Mary Anderson Center, Virginia Center for the Creative Arts, and Ragdale Foundation for their kind and generous support. Special thanks to Sydney and Norman Abend for time in Eastham, to Holly and Fred Hickler, Randi Schalet, Alice McMahon, and Edward Rose for many years of enthusiasm and good advice. Thanks to David Yezzi for choosing this book for the Hollis Summers Prize, and to David Sanders, a kindred poetic spirit and generous editor, for providing this book with its ideal hometown.

For Adine Sagalyn, who gave me Europe,
among other destinations

And for Cecile, my hometown of many years

Contents

A poem begins as a lump in the throat, a sense of wrong, a homesickness, a lovesickness.

—*Robert Frost, in a letter to Louis Untermeyer*

The poem is always in your hometown, but you have a better chance of finding it in another.

—*Richard Hugo, "The Triggering Town"*

Alton Bay Postcard

to Becky Lillian

Sleep fills the houses like a gas.
Whatever flies were caught inside are curled up
on windowsills, filled with a small, dry sleep.
Real estate calendars yellow on August.

The bay's snapshot-blue is just as deep
as when we stopped here thirty years ago—
do you remember? The Winnebago
Cabins beckon. Perhaps we could keep

house here a few weeks next summer.
That local girl we met has left to marry now,
I'm sure, but brings her children back. She'd know
they're more like tourists now, who come here

but forget that, since in her heart the bay's still hers.
Although we were just passing through,
the barbershop quartet sang songs I knew
and I loved her. This was my hometown for an hour.

Evanston Postcard

The elms are dead. The old library's gone.
The war is over in Vietnam.
A sign mentions the Internet
so I can't pretend it's 1968.
The old library had a fireplace with real fires
all winter long. Different songs blare
from radios down at the lake.
Waves pound the beach like a migraine headache.
Do air-raid sirens drill still each Tuesday at ten-
thirty? I thought the garbagemen
were poor but they were only dirty. Petunias were
tornadoes planted by the neighbors
from Greece or Germany, some regime.
At least four countries called our block home.
That maple we planted when my brother was born
no longer swoons in the wind; it's just blank lawn.
I didn't know the P.O. was W.P.A.
How little I knew before we moved away.
I saw the garage where my mother died.
I don't think she knew how her suicide
would change us. How little we remember.
Hometowns trap the past in tiny bits of amber:
the store where shoes were bought each fall; the township pool;
the heady smell of lilacs. Then comes the future's wrecking ball.
I wander streets I walked down then but now
I'm her age, not ten, though I don't know how

that happened. I dreamt this visit anyway.
The real town's stopped, my own Pompeii,
when Chandler's still sold Girl Scout outfits
and Field's was open, making profits.
It's summer. Children play outside.
Time will never reach the day she died.

Winter, Chicago

Winter impounds the waves of Lake Michigan
    With one too-curious child caught in the frozen
Undertow. What I want to see cannot be seen
    From this window, like the clock that once ticked
At the end of my grandfather's telescope.
    The child and the clock are overgrown
By time and buildings. My grandfather is dead.
    He could tell time by the clock on the Wrigley Building,
Twenty-three blocks south in its white gown.
    In my childhood insomnia I could tell
Time by the binary lights of these buildings,
    Punched out like code for a nightmare machine.
For one hundred hours now, it has been sub-zero;
    Since Friday, thirty-six thousand cars have stalled.
Smoke unfurls from the North Side rooftops,
    Wool découpage atop the flat, photographed zones.
The trees below are lassoed with lights,
    Gold constellations blurring the straight avenues.
Snow sits on the shoulders of the statues
    Like the light of grace. A frozen horn ignites.
The barrio darkens, a cold oven.
    Only the snow burns a sweet, blue flame.
My life is a city on the head of a pin:
    Each block rehearses its epicenter,
The horns blare, the caryatids shiver.
    My grandmother and her sister soon will sleep

Through the city's frantic decibels.
　　Though I guard the window like a sentinel,
Death cannot be seen with a telescope,
　　Nor can the child be recovered.

Now sirens wail, a blue codicil.

Lincoln Park Postcard

Chicago, December

Early morning in Lincoln Park. The lake
is a slice of ice-blue truth beneath the gray
horizon. The trees are all still snarled with dark.
Peach-pink streetlights dot the Outer Drive. The glass
conservatory glows, its captured jungle

tangled with shadows. The day's first dog darts
among still-graceful spikes of prairie grass,
oblivious to winter's chilly solstice.
I watch it all from behind the lush cartouche
this building wears like a sphinx's headband.

What if this address weren't just pretending
for a month and the park were always mine —
furry yarrow, foxglove, bee balm, canna,
verbena, columbine; June brides posing
by the fountain, its jets turned on again?

New shifts arrive to guard the sleeping lobbies.
Now the doormen know my name though they'll forget,
like merchants who knew my brand of cigarettes
before I quit. But this city is a habit
I can't break. I'll be back to live along the lake.

Corydon Postcard

Greetings from the old state capital!
I'm camped out on the bandstand at Elm and Beaver
trying to understand the feel of living here forever.
Down at the drugstore soda fountain
I found some true necessities
of Indiana life: windproof Zippos,
Dr. Grabow pre-smoked pipes, paint chips,
communion cards, two plastic swordfish.
(Now all I need's a wife.) Where would I work?
Forever Young? Emporium "Mall"? Indian Creek?
(Or have I gotten married to the soda jerk?)
I think that's me, working at the Goodwill store,
so ingrained by now I know exactly who wore
what before it found its way to the collection box.
There are folks who stop here for a thirty-dollar
rolling pin or other overpriced antiques—
I know they think we're podunk freaks
who don't have network television,
but there's enough to make a life from almost
anywhere: lunch at Jock's; sweet, hungry sex;
bandstand concerts in the summertime; a house
on Cherry; someone to marry; a wake
at the awning'd funeral home. It's enough to make
a life from or at least to make a poem.

Kentuckiana Postcards

to Josh Bloom

1

Hello from Nowhere in Particular,
and yet another town I fell in love with.
It's the usual: the Washeteria, Hubcaps Galore,
Little Chef Diner, not to mention Faith

Liquors. I'm so predictable. All the downtown
buildings need to do is raise their painted eyebrows
slightly or flash old-fashioned neon and I'm gone
(like making wedding plans on the first date). I browse

for next year's calendar ("THEY'RE IN!") though it's July
and get my shoe size checked ("IT CHANGES YEAR TO YEAR").
I must find out if they serve Jell-O
here (or it could never work). The theater

is closed, of course, though you can buy appliances
and furniture ("TENT SALE TODAY!"), and the jeweler's
still open. (But where can I get the fiancée
to buy them for?) Am I a fool or

what, to think love and towns like this should last
forever? One more walk by the river
and I know I must go, like the ghosts unkissed
in the balcony while the screen below flickers with lovers.

2

Yup, another place whose curlicues and neon
and blank marquee seduced me. (If I paid dues
at every Odd Fellows' I've photographed . . .)
But I worried that the waitress hated Jews

it took so long to get my order
(and she had tattoos) till I saw she was just
nervous. (Turns out she's very new here.)
One by one, the other diners confessed

to me how far away they've been from Indiana—
Boston, Seattle, thirteen years in New York—
in an ironic contest one trucker supplied
mileage for. Then each explained why he'd come back,

as if I'd somehow disapprove of that.
I, in turn, pretended I was *from* somewhere,
though after twenty years I still get called a "breezer."
I couldn't say, "I want to be a regular

in every town like this—each street seems so
evocative of all the lives I could have led—"
like the one where I run the public library,
the one in which my mother hadn't died,

and one in the last century, when I was
(can you imagine it?) the haberdasher's bride.
The life where I have children, the one
in which I'll never go abroad, and read

the Bible daily. The life where I work
at Little Chef and serve my other self the tea
(the four-refill limit would not apply to me),
the one in which instead of *go,* I'd *stay.*

Postcard to Robin in Kent, Ohio

1990

Your postmark brings back the pavement's bloody Rorschach
immortalized (like the *Challenger*'s ideogram)
by a photo History keeps in its scrapbook.
We met six years after Kent State. Vietnam

was already fading from the map. I was
seventeen, already older than the girl who screamed
over that boy's dead body; you, in your twenties,
older than the boy ever would be. Even that time

seems over now, its hope; the Hundred Flowers
Café — or was it Bookstore? — where we met long gone. . . .
Is there a monument or do the powers
that be prefer to forget what was done

there? No doubt they do. I too would like to forget
1970, my mother's suicide
six weeks before Kent State's random target
practice. She was thirty-eight when she died,

younger than you now, with the ghosts in Ohio.
Since then, your sister has died by the same
method. At least they *wanted* to die,
unlike those four kids the Guards didn't even aim

at; isn't that better? . . . God, what triggered these thoughts?
Oh, yes, the postmark on your letter, the name

of a town I've never even been to, its shots
heard 'round the world the same as Concord's . . . Blame

won't bring any of them back. Their wars are over.
I'm sure the students out there never take cover
now except when it rains, a lesson uncanny
in its relevance for both you and your old friend, Jenny.

Cape House

for the Abends

A chime of some sort tinkles next door
like a sweet calf's cowbell. Wind brushes the dune's hair
distractedly, pausing sometimes as if to stare
into the bay's half-silvered mirror. Nothing is there.

The moon, with its squashed newborn head, is asleep
and the gulls have gone wherever gulls go
when they are not eating or laughing.
(Sometimes I've seen them way down the beach,

sitting, round and huge as some extinct thing's eggs,
until my approach hatches them.) A frog
visits here nightly, leaping at the windows
like a child at Christmas shop displays.

He reminds me of myself, trying to get in
to the lemony light, the syrup of home
at night. Wellfleet's electric constellations
begin to wink almost merrily the orange

pink of distant bonfires. Huddled together
they look like the lights of a gambling ship
anchored offshore. Night is a velvet barge
that fills the harbor. Wellfleet's lights are

also votives lit for its fleet of black boats
that trawl the bay daily. The July

after my mother died, my cousins and I
lit the beach with dozens of sparklers—

candles on the medieval cakes of sandcastles
we'd made. For them it was just another way
to celebrate the holiday. For me
it was building a city that still had joy

in it. Beneath the bay's gray waves, hermit crabs
kept changing homes, as I would many times
after that summer. Low tide splayed out
its interesting assortment of things,

interpretable like the I Ching,
though I had no key to their meanings then.
Sun glinted off boats like decoder rings
but I could not tell if the gulls were laughing

or crying. Two decades have fortified
the dunes though not my heart. Home is still
a tidal flat, unbuildable: one minute,
a drained moat; then cormorants poke up

their periscope necks from its depths
like a cartographer's sea monster.
How shall I live? Wellfleet's lamps are lit,
rose gold estate jewelry I'll never inherit,

and I've nothing to prove I'm more than a tourist
here—or anywhere, really. Way out in the bay
Jeremy Point's lights flash red and green,
like some small town's lone intersection

guiding phantom traffic all night, and Billingsgate
Island's buried foundations lie shipwrecked
beneath the waves, like the towns they drowned
to make the Quabbin Reservoir out west.

I hear there are reunions of the residents
whose towns the government flooded, a kind
of club to mourn coming from somewhere
that doesn't exist anymore except in their minds

and a few sepia photographs. Grief like that
surrounds me the way water did when I walked out
to Jeremy Point and the tide came in.
Tonight's tide has tiptoed in, not wanting

to wake anyone, though I'm here alone
waiting up for its reassuring step
on the beach and then its hush-hush in my ear
like a kind lover's sweet breath as we sleep.

What made me swim to land that day I stood
stranded on the last patch of sand out there
in the bay? I'd hiked to the Point because
it had haunted my sight so long—I'd even tried

to paint it—and I wanted to visit
a place so often imagined it was as strong
as memory, like my phantom home.
Of course it was just sand. I found this house

with my binoculars—the fat chimney
and eel grass lawn, the many windows

I'd looked out of at the very horizon
I now stood poised on. Had I left on a light,

some beacon to my self, a sparkler
stalled like the light of stars for years
before it reaches here? No one waited for me—
no mother or lover, no cousins all grown now,

not my lost father. Only the poem
I hadn't written yet beckoned me back
as the sea tightened its dark vignette
around each ankle like the end of an old film. . . .

And now it is done. I sit again
in this borrowed home, a fire crackling
like old typewriters clacking, the bay mine
for a weekend. Deadbeat hermit crabs

move out again, avoiding rent this time
entirely, as I've avoided love's
long mortgage. The foghorn is silent
like Waltham's broken church bells or voices

I won't hear again. No mist will make
those voices boom; no scaffolding can resurrect
their hours. Their only home is where I go,
far from the sea's sweet undertow.

Cape Cod Postcard

The map of the Cape flexes its muscles.
Manomet bulges—biceps to P-town's
curled fist. Inlets ripple like arterial
highways. I am here alone, in the off-season.

The hermit crabs and I have found
a hundred vacancies—unheated—and hope
to last the weekend without crying. The wind's
baritone is the only culture left here; it gropes

for the grass's high notes in the rain.
I've strained to hear the foghorn's boyish tenor
but it's gone, like the tourists' noisy children.
Will they remember it, as I have all these years—

the ocean's rooster—or was it just another
summer for them? Today I braved the beach
to watch cold fishermen in waders
casting off. What is it like to watch

the water not for metaphors, but fish?
I see the ocean's muddy hemline rising
like the tide of Paris fashions, or wish
I were a boat in the crook of Orleans'

arm. I hear of stranded pilot whales
at First Encounter Beach and think of love. . . .
So, who said poets should be practical?
I hope this finds you well when it arrives.

Metaphors at Low Tide

The tide bows out like an obsequious servant
till sand flats stretch, vast as the floor
of a janitor's nightmare. Clumps of green fleece
are wet mops gone clammy—again, his bad dream.

Careful as a Jain with no one to sweep for him,
I tiptoe among the periwinkles.
Hermit crabs scurry like tow trucks
around the snails' stalled traffic.

In the world of their puddle it is all
so purposeful! Gulls, which earlier dropped clam-bombs
on the beachhead, are calm now—Victorian women
wading, or penguins on their tundra.

What am I to them, I wonder? Cumulus?
Colossus? Or are they less curious
than I am, examining these razor clams
ditched by hoodlums when they heard the foghorn's siren?

Straw surf—dried eel grass—breaks along the beach.
Miles of sand marcelled by wind pantomime
the waves which brought that silent surf here.
No undertow is safer. Drained, the bay's

a closet opened up to show a child
no monster lurks there; filled, the darkness irks her still
with fears she can't explain. To calm her, then,
the tide—a patient mother—goes out yet again.

Postcard from Herring Brook Road

for Vanda Sendzimir

High tide marbleizes the salt marsh,
the bay's elegant endpaper, while a breeze
swirls in its ruffles and shadows.
Gulls blow around like whole sections of news-

print no one will read now. A red-winged blackbird
flashes by. His colors saturate the air,
lush as Sunday's rotogravures. Wind in the trees
is made of taffeta and does not tear. . . .

One Scotch pine's candelabras—like sconces
from a hundred torn-down Roxies—transform
the marsh to a movie's vast proscenium,
the endless stage of Thirties musicals, too enorm-

ous to be real. Dawn's chorus girls rehearse
at random—sweet chaos, not cacophony.
A few herons audition for extras'
positions with the corps de ballet

while fiddler crabs sit in their orchestra pit
till the union rep tells them to play. (Or are they
a marching band at some cancelled game,
the soggy field in disarray, each heavy claw

a tuba that can't be put away?) The bay
seems merely metaphor—the backdrop

for a grade-school *Pinafore*, dry as the whitecaps
buoying Botticelli's Venus on her scallop.

I'm used to it close up—its waves bathing my feet
like priests at Easter—but just this once
I'm grateful for the distance, and respite
from its deep and dark persistence.

Eastham Postcard

Cicadas sizzle in Sunken Meadow.
Crickets chirp like newborn foghorns.
The sky blots up sunset the way the tide
takes footprints. Dusk always makes me mourn.

Cars' lights cut through the night, mute locomotives.
Their opal stares match the moon's yellow hair.
The drive-in's skyglow makes nostalgia's bonfire flare.
Even dunes are going gray this year.

Wires stretch — unwritten music — down the road.
Constellations fill in crickets' notes.
Bullfrogs seem to strum the staff itself
while birds sing arias in quotes.

Too late to learn the drive-in's plot.
Too soon to swim, the tide's not in.
"Too late too soon," a gull's cry warns.
Fiddler crabs play while August burns.

Sunken Meadow Postcard

Eastham

Crickets creak quickly, desperate and doomed,
while the foghorn booms its serene *om, om,*
at the other extreme of fall's metronome.
Dozens of birds perch on the utility lines—
dense notes of a score I'd never try to learn.
Goldenrod bold as fishermen's slickers
brightens the meadow. Soon rain will lacquer
the deck and I'll go. For now I'm a kid
alone in the neighborhood after school's started—
the meadow, *all mine;* the bay, *all mine;* Wellfleet's bluffs
awaiting some Impressionist painter, *mine too.* Life's
fine for a moment. The gull blowing past is a sign.
Whitecaps cross the beach's finish line.

Off-Season

The rain tells knock-knock jokes. Spiders batten
down the doors. Goldenrod keeps its lights on
all day, a funeral cortège as long
as a president's. One particular
cricket sings distinctly, close by. He is
Ishi, the pure voice of summer before tourists.
Butterflies flutter like the last load of laundry
hung out to dry. The beach looks littered
with summer people's broken furniture
but it is just the tide's huge ideograms.
Wind, which starched the neighbors' flag, now pleats
the water into waves like a waiter
folding fancy napkins. The restaurant
will close though the waves continue,
eternity's assembly-line like the one
weekenders escaped from.
The neighbors have returned to Florida,
where they are winter people.
Gulls gossip, but only about locals.
Already the crickets have begun to sound like sleigh bells.

Provincetown Postcard

Christmas lights tattoo Commercial Street's
half-closed facades—odd, how seaside life
goes on in winter like the future
of some high school friend you never thought of
later, who by now has got two daughters
and a second wife. The street's deserted,
as if a villain and the sheriff were
about to shoot it out, though nobody
peers from behind these shutters
except the endless pairs of sunglasses
staring toward June. Eight o'clock.
A church bell and one foghorn sing an aria
so poignant I want to cry. The marina
swizzles its lights into the harbor.
It's Tuesday. I must be the last tourist
in P-town. How paradoxical "home" is—
you must get sick of it to earn the right
to have to stay in spite of that. I've never been
able to take any place for granted
like these year-rounders I see scratching
their lottery tickets at the Governor Bradford.
Where would they go with their winnings?
How do we know where we belong? Already
I've eavesdropped—twice—in one café, copping
local gossip as if I might stay here
long enough to make it pay. It's not as though
I had no anchor elsewhere. No, in fact,
they drop so readily it scares me.

Am I some hysterical patient who sops up
others' symptoms like so much gravy
or just someone with too many
epicenters, like the bar scene here in July?
Neither comparison comforts me much.
Sometimes I just want to be able to touch
one place on the map like a lover's breast
and say that's where my heart is. Which name
would I shout in the middle of passion? Which town
should I marry? Or is love arbitrary,
like where we're born? The foghorn honks distractedly,
a bored cabby, impatient for his fare
but paid to wait, who can't complain about his fate
of unknown destinations any more
than I can. It got me here, at any rate.

East End Postcard

Provincetown, December

I love the mosaic these shacks make
as they gerrymander the air for their views
of the harbor. Some tiptoe on stilts
right down to the water, precarious
as drag queens in Fifties stilettos.
An unleashed Labrador studies the jetties.
Laundry lines shiver with year-rounders' skivvies.
At night Route 6 wears a fabulous topaz
necklace on the décolleté bay, the marina,
a tiara of lights near where I stay.
What life might I live were I brave enough
to love the right woman? Hourly all of us fall
in the circle of P-town's sole church bell—
the gulls, quaint cottages of lovers, and me.
Time has no tourists, unlike the sea,
or love, although unwillingly.

The Storm

Provincetown

Last night's rain fell as thick as Gettysburg's volleys
all turned one way, piercing the harbor

like the flesh of fifty thousand soldiers.
High tide bleeds into the street this morning

though there is no moaning here, not even gulls
keening, whinnying, insanely laughing—

the whole shrill gamut of their repertoire.
Where do gulls go during the sky's shooting season?

It's over now, anyway; the fog's too thick
to hit anything on purpose. The widow's walks

are empty, though for a different reason:
No one returns. And the widows are dead.

The foghorn booms and a church bell chimes back—
danger and time tuning to the same pitch.

Why must they die so young—those soldiers,
this town's gaunt men, people I love?

Teach me, teach me the utility of anguish,
how the bell and foghorn learn each other's language.

Postcard from Herring Cove Beach

Provincetown

I watch the beach from my head-on parking space
like a drive-in movie or *Video Fireplace*.
It's December. None of the topless lesbians
I've heard so much about are here, of course;
summer's mermaids retire to prows of ships
and other cities. The lighthouse has
no one to wink at now except a few sailors
immune to its charms. Cormorants dive and surface,
submarines drilling during the Cold War's
off-season. How many of the water's
other admirers today are locals, I wonder—
or is it too cliché, too busman's holiday,
to come here and stare at the ocean, as I do?
Would you get blasé, trading its trinkets
all summer? Gulls blow away like taffy wrappers
no one's left to litter. Plymouth rises
across the bay. Behind me, Provincelands'
strange dunes loom like a lunar golf course.
(Imagine golf with turned-off gravity—
like love, I suppose, without mortality.)
A phantom rowboat—seal or whale?—capsizes.
A Coast Guard chopper trawls the air,
above it all yet unaware.

Route 1 Postcard

California

The ocean's left hand reaches out for its right one.
Waves crack on rocks like knuckles. Nothing pacific
about these breakers. Progressively, Route 1
goes color-blind—blue, green, and black
are all there is. Yellow shouts then shock
the scenic traveler: some Alpine bloom, pure sun
leaked out of Proserpine's eclipse. A wreck
would go unnoticed here, like her abduction.

El Camino's colonial bell won't clang
this high, where oblivious cows hang off
breathtaking cliffs and the ocean's
truth is so profound no poem could dwarf it.
Trying to frame it, I'm reminded of the sight
of flashcubes popping off the Empire State at night.

Menlo Park Postcard

to Elizabeth Alexander

Sunday morning outside of San Francisco.
Anonymous pink plants animate the stucco
houses. Dawn is the pastel of Deco

paint so common here. A little homesick,
I look around for lyric things to comfort me. I pick
a cyclamen—so real after L.A.'s generic

blooms and, best of all, I know its name.
I miss that most, so far from home, though I have come
for it. Next door, a dryer starts to hum

and someone whose name I'll never know
begins her day. The namelessness of hobos
now occurs to me. How long could I go

on this way? I think of all the towns
I know my way around—though none as green
as this—and wonder if I'd trade them in

for wanderlust. By now sun must have graced
the Bridge's red meridians and Angel Island's rainbow lost
its glow. Only tourists will have eaten breakfast

in their zest to see what citizens will miss.
I compromise: no photos of mysterious
redwood forests; I've stayed inside instead and written this.

Mt. San Angelo Postcard

Virginia

Cicadas here work overtime, three shifts
of buzz saws building some imaginary high-rise.
A primal rooster crows, lackadaisical
about the hour like good vacationers.
Ailanthus wears its sporrans, as if dressed
for some parade, and the corn has put its aigrets on.
One mockingbird trades songs like baseball cards.
Underfoot, a million crickets hiccup.
Two cows chew clover daintily, quaint ladies
out for salad and a tête-à-tête.
Blue mountains loom abroad, the muses' Ararat.
At night the fireflies' lights, flickering
like half-remembered words, decorate
the lawn's elaborate garden party. A few birds
sing late, most lyric after all the garden's guests have gone,
while the moon watches, accidentally left on.

Country Headache

Sunrise smears on its lipstick, bleary.
Crickets bang out a hangover
on their toy piano. The cicadas'
rude construction crew begins too early.
("But, lady, the boss man told us to . . .")
One mockingbird surfs stations constantly,
searching for his favorite song, over and over.
("How can he dare . . . ?" the wild grape rages,
in her kimono and unkempt hair.)
Sick of the din, day gulps the moon
like a single, scrounged-for aspirin.
So much it cannot cure . . .
Spent lilies—chickens with their heads cut
off—stagger in the wind, still throbbing . . .
till butterflies bandage the air.

Country Erotica

Butterflies flutter like lingerie
left out to dry and to tantalize a little.
The thistles' purple nipples harden.
A gawky wasp wields his stinger awkwardly,
like a teenager's perpetual hard-on.
The plantains' phalli climb like the silly towers
of San Gimignano. Just call me Ruth
among the corn's erections. I want
to run my hands through the fescue's whiskers
and kudzu's let-down hair. My mouth
remembers where the roses were.
Chicory electrifies the air.
Crickets throb with sex's iambics.
Cicadas—in see-through negligees—
try to synchronize their sizzling too.
No one doubts the crow's O–O–O
as it echoes across the meadow.
Now the wild rye's velvet spikelets droop, half-soft,
and a snake sloughs off its skin (some designer condom).
Frogs seem to purr. Dusk's breath is slow.
I bask in the fireflies' afterglow.

Country Holiday

Hundreds of birds have just perched
in the Osage orange's branches
like a department store's
overdecorated Christmas tree.

The ornate, vermiculated fruit—
skin a green mezzotint
of its smooth orange cousin's—
hangs like avant-garde ornaments

the buyer bought too many of.
Squirrels circle below—toy trains—
and butterflies flurry their fake snow
here and there for effect.

I'm glad it's July
so I can just enjoy it,
glad I'm a Jew
and there's nothing to buy.

Night Train

for Abby Robinson and Star Black

Fireflies flare: hobos' struck matches.
Moonlight's steel wool shines the tracks. A dog barks.
Darkness licks the semaphores' red lollipops.
There's no stop here, where kudzu drapes the trees'

tall furniture like years of cobwebs.
No ticket's necessary not to go
anywhere except the place a train whistle can
take you. Tree frogs chitter. Cicadas

wind down. The night's all percussion.
Novices are fooled by the trucks' ventriloquism
from Route 29, and hope those distant headlights
are the train, but it is just another pickup

trawling the dark lane. Stars come out,
dim and distant as an alphabet
one cannot read yet. Why do we wait here
night after night, with no luggage but flashlights

to hail the engineer and sometimes, perhaps,
a six-pack of beer? A stopped clock's right twice
each day. Sometimes it's best to stay somewhere
to learn about leaving. That's why *I* wait, anyway.

Then it's here and we're deer caught in its stare
or soldiers mugging for a last picture

before marching off to war, framed, intent,
an elegy for the same moment. . . .

Some nights, when the lights are on and shades are up,
the train casts a snakeskin shadow into the ditch,
molting, trying to wriggle past itself.
How well I understand that struggle!

The engineer rewards us with his whistle —
harmonica played on nostalgia's Victrola —
a sound that makes the air immortal, like the air
in dreams. But the train churns on to New Orleans.

The caboose winks like a last rushed guest
stumbling after departing friends, his thanks
called back in vain. A moment of silence.
Then moonlight shines the tracks again.

Victoriana

Sweet Briar, Virginia

Cicadas wind up summer's clock.
Crickets practice chamber music.
Asters swirl their parasols
and pity all the poorer souls.

What frock will July wear today
and would she like fog's tulle or not?
The cardinal's livery—just *outré!*
(At least that's what the house wren thought.)

Breezes mailed with one-cent stamps
deliver news of just-mown lawns
where cattle graze and children dance
till fireflies come to light the lamps.

Southern Postcard

Ten thousand white-gloved dogwood butlers usher us
through the South. Their black skins itch in livery,
their bent waists ache with slavery,
till June—not Lincoln—sets them free. But one has tossed
his gloves down, see? Visions of Montgomery.

History and wisteria. Star-crossed
flag of the Confederacy. Every-
where bronze members of the cavalry
guard their public square. Did Appomatox
happen yet? And who surrendered—Grant or Lee?

Gettysburg Postcard

Dusk cloaks the sky in Rebel gray—a Union spy
whose blue day will prevail though fifty thousand die
here. Their dogwood ghosts surrender every spring.
Fog scouts the woods in moccasins
then blows away like cannon smoke—that easily
they died. How odd that we can ride here now
and worship at weird obelisks the future
has installed to say goodbye. The fields are
their own monument: no souvenir but silence—
our taste of what the soldiers got on these same lawns.
The trees wear mossy uniforms
to camouflage their shame, and each one takes the name
of one who died. These famous acres, Lincoln said,
made heroes of the dead, and more blood would be shed
to prove his claim. Did liberty inspire them?
I couldn't say. I think they never would have come
knowing what we know today—
how grim the outcome that July
and Appomatox years away.

Appomatox Postcard

Hiroshima Day, 1993

All day I searched for similarities:
Flamingo lawn ornaments along Route 60
became pink cranes folded by a thousand Sadakos
for luck. The pines were scribbled in awkward kanji.

The radio's Southern voices were as weird to me
as Hirohito's was to commoners
when they first heard him speak—on air,
of Japan's surrender. Grant and Lee

spoke of Mexico for half an hour
before they even mentioned Lee's surrender,
polite as Tokyo businessmen. But the war—
I was stunned to learn—did not end here:

only Lee's men laid down their muskets—
or, rather, propped them up into teepees,
like some grim ikebana of épées. No peace
was wrought for any other Confederates,

who fought on elsewhere, the South's unlucky
kamikazes. They just became more faceless Japs,
whose deaths then etched on local maps
the nineteenth century's Nagasakis. . . .

Virginia Postcard

for Patricia Elam

Today the crickets' singing is hundreds
of schoolmarms ringing their bells or the sound
of a distant car alarm. Incessant
cicadas rattle like African gourds

whose medicine did not work here. Some days
they whisper like the mist of sprinklers left on
by a gardener, turning the air patrician
as surely as the sound of lobbed tennis balls does.

Yesterday I went to Appomatox.
No monuments anywhere condemned the war.
Daughters of the Confederacy had left fresh flowers
and flags for their heroes. (I suppose German attics

are full of swastikas.) I wept for the one
Union soldier buried there. Now the crepe myrtles
will not offer me their handkerchiefs. Swallowtails
will not curtsy to me as they chaperone

the lawn's cotillion, still wearing elaborate
mourning for sons lost at Manassas and Bull Run.
Kudzu drools over everything, a veteran
no one wants home anymore. . . . As I write,

two buzzards soar, black kites flown by a lonely boy
from the North. A white steeple empties its quiet
syringe into the sky. Somewhere men quote
Hitler for their next war's alibi.

Lipik Postcard

Croatia, Yugoslavia, 1982

Lipik's graveyard is lush as tropics,
blushing a hundred wet blooms,
the village women tending them.

A vendor sent me to this garden,
directing me in perfect Deutsch
and promising that I could reach

the grave of Alfred Miller,
my great-grandfather,
son of the village innkeeper,

who died hiding, running
with partisans, his yellow star on,
shot near the war's end by Nazis (Croatian).

Across from the vendor's kiosk
was the mustard-colored inn,
its name worn thin—so thin

one more rain might have ruined it.
But genealogy resists
the picturesque: no grave exists

for Alfred here, there's nothing
I can make bloom like these women can,
pumping and watering all afternoon.

Only one grave here has been forgotten:
a German grave, overgrown with weeds
and buried behind three feet

of dried vines. One evergreen
is the cenotaph I claim.
The tulips' goblets now toast Alfred's name.

Letter from Orahovica

Croatia, July 19, 1941

Earlier that day he was with us as we posed in the field at dawn for a photograph, as we smoked and shaved by the river, as we burned every house in the village. I don't recall his step but his aim was always accurate. When the captain called us, he was neither first nor last in line.

Click, click. Hans's camera framed the partisans we'd caught, propped up against the massive haystack, joined at their clammy hands like cut-outs, identical in their blindfolds. We waited until Hans stepped back. The captain gave his terse command, off-hand as a rich man ordering his car. (This was to let the peasants know how unimportant they were.) Josef—Schultz—seemed not to have heard the captain's quick *Bereit!* and stood dreaming with a shell-shocked look. *Ready*, the captain called again, this time bitter, impatient, not for the prisoners' benefit, but as if he knew what was coming. Josef stared but did not move. The air smelled of smoke and hay and sweat. The captain questioned. Josef put down his gun. The captain made threats. Josef began to undress—helmet, cartridge belt, all the signs. Then he was through and walked toward the haystack. After four steps, he turned back, dropped his dog-tag into his helmet. Not one of us had dropped his gun from his shoulder. Then Josef took his place in the other line.

The next man in the other line, though blindfolded and unable to understand German, took Josef's hand, making a last friend. Hans's clicking sounded like a bloodless gun. Josef stared and did not say a word. The captain made a sign and then a low sound. The peasants leaped forward, obedient as dolls. Josef still stood, friendless; none of us had shot him. Hans clicked. One of the peasants gurgled. The captain quickly ordered fire and Josef was dead. Then the captain took his pistol and fired two more shots into Josef's head.

Mostar Postcard

Bosnia-Hercegovina, Yugoslavia, 1982

Soldiers on holiday fill the outdoor café.
A young man has just jumped off the old bridge
for their money, on his chest a tattoo
of their leader, a hero hired by heroes.
These men are the same age as I am
but theirs is the age of the native-born,
drawn on their handsome faces with a dark pen.
Peasants, mechanics, farmers—I would not dare
to call them brothers. One winks. Some stare.
I pretend to look at the river.
How war makes borders glamorous,
our time brief and historic!
But this is not war, just the face of war;
not love, just faces of lovers.
Love could launch Mostar's minarets—
love, or war—though language stops us here:
dawdling at the river's edge
where history whispers in each soldier's ear.

Hampstead Postcard

England

The blurry moon means rain.
Three poplars burn, black flames.
This balcony's serene,
that Jaguar quite tame.

Roses clamor at Marx's tomb
while Mary Ann Evans looks on.
John Keats's rooms welcome pilgrims
but the nightingale is gone.

Volleyed birdies mine the lawn.
The neighbors' pool-sweep mimes
a swan. Cook calls everyone
first names and wears no uniform.

The Heath is where I go to dream.
(Decorum mums the garden.)
How long before trees lose their claim?
The skyline's teeth keep coming in.

Washington, D.C., Postcard

1988, for my NEA co-workers

November inaugurates December,
passing on Washington Monument's
baton. October's umber disappears,
its leaves like money spent on war.
The crickets, out of office now, repent.

Lincoln ponders the Potomac, penniless
himself, another frozen park-bench tenant.
Winter re-elects a congress
of compatriots to fill the tourists' vacancies.
They line the Mall, campaign funds spent,

poverty's incumbents. Tonight's bus fills
with fellow bureaucrats, intent
on some disaster just averted — not global,
but secretarial. Their clocks repeal
the hours until each weekend. They used to want

to change the world. . . . Snow begins another
filibuster. (The president has vetoed spring
this year.) My stint here is nearly over,
like an ambassador recalled before
she's learned most local acronyms or slang,

but not too soon to call the country home. O, my
Emerald City made for black-and-white TV,
which a thousand field trips thrill to see,
I have fallen in love with my enemy.
(May someone grant me clemency!)

Harvard Square Postcard

The Square is gray as bus exhaust today.
Almost August, at the café Impressionists
might have frequented till the cliché

of their arrangement changed cheap breakfasts
into trends; as if imagination
could be franchised. Sparrows I've almost

come to recognize beg their morning's ration.
The pigeons' coos are more rhetorical,
like horns in traffic jams or conversation

among the café regulars. I envy all
the waitresses, whose conversations can be
practical, who can remain anonymous and fall

in love. Fiction suits them perfectly:
anything can happen but not happen—
make love with her, dance with him; next day

begin from scratch, anonymous and un-
attached. Poetry and I are less promiscuous,
though I'd switch genres for a few of these patrons.

But the plaza's filling up with strangers. Work is close
as the kiosk's news of it. The church's slate-
gray steeple sports its weathervane, staunch as any cross,

and Summer mugs the office workers. Heaven sweats
its dross of rain as customers disperse —
another morning rescued from its debt.

Back Bay Postcard

Brahmin boudoirs gentrify the night.
Below my feet the Indians once fished.
Magnolias reupholster these staid streets each spring.
Time passes like checks the rich needn't cash.

April's arrived, chauffeured by March.
The tulips are filled with helium.
Sconces decant the wine-colored rooms.
I want every address to be my home.

My Boston grandmother must also have walked here,
window-shopping for class like a lunch-hour
dowager or one of my grandfather's cab fares.
Is my envy less ugly than hers

since I *could* have the beauty I crave
but refuse? A dog, reckless with unleashed
joy, zigzags the long allée of trees
clasping the Emerald Necklace like Paris

with grass and alphabetical cross streets,
though an alley would make him as happy.
The swan boats float empty in their lagoon,
as if Grammy and I might ride them again.

Bay State Road

Magnolias unclench their fleshy fists
(when "flesh" was a Caucasian crayon).
Spring is fresh sap dabbed at their wrists.
Irises untwist like lipstick or a barber's sign.

I love this street—its many languages of flowers
and kerchief'd sidewalk-sweepers, their brooms
whisking away the pollen dribbled everywhere
like face powder scattered in Nature's dressing room

and the dogwood petals underfoot like popcorn
kernels after a movie. Ivy shimmies
up the vast side wall of the last brownstone.
When it shimmers, I think of the lamé

on a flapper's gown. Two doors down in June
wisteria will curl into young girls'
ringlets and the tiny shrine of roses begin
to bloom. Now scullers on the nearby Charles

rehearse their sweaty regatta with staccato
strokes that barely ruffle the surface
of the river's blue legato.
Each day, as I walk to my airshaft office—

where the carpet is no new-mown lawn
and the ringing phone's more pigeon than robin—
I think: in spite of that and no matter the season,
what a lucky street to have a job on!

Mackinac Island Postcard

to Martin Edmunds and Carol Moldaw

Friends—
        Queen Victoria is not gone! We overlook
two lakes and lilac'd lawns. No one walks:
one promenades. We came by horse-drawn carriage
in the rain. A few girls wear floral frocks.
Concerts in the parlor are lit by candelabra.
Waitresses in lace pour demitasse
from a silver samovar, and there's local
whitefish caviar. The musicians play
old repertoire. Croquet, anyone?
It's too cool for the cerulean swimming pool
but fine for the filigree of the fountain's
liquid fleur-de-lis. The lawn chairs' heads are
toward Eternity. Yes, time travel is
for me. Greetings from the last century.

Vermont Postcard

Sunset on Lake Champlain
is a blue and sodium-pink affair—
something in common with lustreware
(though nothing garish—more like a scene
by Maxfield Parrish). I've come to "commune
with nature" but when I see the bell-buoys' flashing lights
flickering like a firefly's come-on,
I know that all I'm really looking for is art.

Holsteins rearrange their puzzle pieces patiently,
trying to get it right. I can almost taste
burst cattails' last sweet bite like cotton candy.
Brown buds perch on the sumac's branches, stone finches.
Old fences squat in ideograms about a private hurt.
(Even the woods here know some Robert Frost by heart.)
Have I come to sow or come to reap? Don't know.
May there still be many miles before I sleep.

Niagara Falls Postcard

Greetings from the capital of love,
whose cataracts a punster might foretell.
Next time we come we'll plan for a motel:
one afternoon is simply not enough.

Where other tourists see the Bridal Veil,
I watch the ghosts of buffalos herded off
a thousand cliffs by hunters. Gulls circle as if
they were white buzzards. They wait to no avail.

Sorry to be cynical, I buy
some souvenirs—small TV sets with slides of all
the sights in living color. The primal
screams are missing. The hunters had their alibi

but what is mine? Can I love a girl
afraid of every honeymoon's cheap thrills,
like holding hands in public or acting like a fool?
Yours, of course, until Niagara Falls.

Buffalo Postcard

Snow sweetens the rooftops of this city
where more millionaires lived once upon a time
than anywhere. Steel leaves its sooty
legacy elsewhere now. Poverty redeems
the coupons here (though one can see the seedy
avenues with grandeur in them easily—*grandes dames*
who lived beyond their means for love).
Robin Hood would feel at home in this locale.
Do you believe the town was named *Beau Fleuve*
before bewildered bison became the local
mascot and white men wrecked the river's laugh
with their canal? Typical, *n'est-ce pas?* Your Buffalo Gal.

Delaware Park Postcard

Buffalo, New York

A willow wears its hair the way Phyllis Diller
did, its yellow wig too weird for Delaware
Park's air of Edwardian grandeur. Dried weeds tear
like the lace of old dresses. Last summer

we paddled boats here where skaters soon will scribble
their cursive. But summer is over like a war
whose casualties now bore the public. Though I care
I cannot fix what the equinox made rubble.

Joggers stagger past the closed casino
whose Jazz Age days I like to imagine
as I walk around the lake, aching
with losses bigger than any wager made there. I know

I must go on. Brown loosestrife braids the air
with its dry reflection of mermaids' hair.
Thistles guard the lake's cracked mirror
like miles of barbed wire crocheted to snare

Narcissus from his dark oasis and
me from despair. . . . Dearest, any city I had
planned would have a place like this. We'd promenade
as dusk descends, though in that place you'd take my hand.

Two Postcards from Forest Lawn Cemetery

Buffalo, New York

1

I browse among masons and veterans;
Elks; the first woman architect; a thousand
FATHERS and MOTHERS, none of them mine.
Leaves pack the graves with their excelsior
like boxes of Victorian knickknacks.
What spectacular excess! One man's weighed
down beneath ninety tons of Carrara marble!
It's November, but warm. A few maples
still burn with flames that seem to defoliate
the obelisks, whose forest of smooth, hard
erections soothes me somehow, their lusty
boldness the best cure for dust's coldness. . . .

2

This place is like my favorite kind of town:
its old facades not yet torn down;
the neighbors not nameless, and always around.
I hear the sound of Spoon River's conversations
if I listen to the ground long enough.
A hearse passes. Yes, I'm a woman alone
on a lawn, half-hearing voices. Some promise
peace and no more losses. Squirrels twirl
around trees, revolving like barbers' stripes
in sepia cities. At home here
more than anywhere, I could wait until dawn
but the obelisks' streetlights would never go on.

Prairie Postcard

for Josie Kearns

Spiderwort, Culver's root and bergamot—
the field is full of references no one will get.
A stand of more familiar poplars slants
into the creek, where the local heron let me have a glance
of him. I've come here every day these past two weeks
and sought him like an omen. My deer-filled walks
among the waving prairie dock and purple haze
of frowsy cow parsnip have turned up jays,
the lyric trochees of a couple chickadees,
cardinals, red-winged blackbirds and a band of crows,
but not the heron. That is, until today
and my last walk on the prairie.
Then there he was, wading demurely, waiting for me.
I love the awkward grace of herons, half ballet,
half prehistoric hinges. It was a brief
encounter, just long enough to wonder before he took off,
what does he mean anyway? Is he a sign
of God? A consolation prize? Some trip a fortune-
teller prophesies without its destination
or duration included in her explanation
of your life? Last night's Tarot turned up The Lovers.
Above me for a moment, the heron hovers.

Lake Forest Postcard

to C.M.P.

Crows squawk each morning like dogs barking back
and forth, waking me up. I'm homesick.
I walk a lot. Yesterday I stalked a heron
as he waded up the creek while I remained
half a block behind—a burka'd wife resigned
to all fate had assigned her. Today
I took my guidebook to the field and tried
to match the flowers with photos there.
My jackpot came whenever a flower and photo tied—
a slot machine whose payoff was a single name.
Poplars waved their white-gloved leaves like royalty.
A viceroy pumped its bellows then became the flame.
White butterflies flapped dollhouse sheets above the flower heads
like Goldilocks looking for the right size bed.
(I thought of you in our bed and your lovely face,
your breasts beneath a negligee of Queen-Anne's lace.
The coneflowers' nipples aren't as nice as yours,
whose rosehip ripens likes its metaphors.
Oh, to lie with you in meadows no one mows,
wrapped up in prairie calicos!)
"*Tsk, tsk,*" say the cicadas of my homesickness
and wasted life. Blue jays laugh about my endless
grief. Fireflies, on the other hand, understand
my loneliness; they sting the dark with sudden pangs
of it. Crickets tick like clocks set out to comfort
just-weaned puppies and soothe me as your breathing does,
wind sieved through screens, waves smoothing sand

in tony suburbs all along the lake. Darling,
whatever it was I came for escapes me now.
All that's left to do here is to ache.

Ragdale Postcard

Lake Forest, Illinois

Vinca drips from my window box
like a leaky faucet. Lipstick-pink geraniums
keep bubbling up. Water plops into the fountain's
basin like endless grapes into gaping mouths

of lazy Romans. Chickadees *see–saw* the air.
Crows bicker and I just listen
from my wicker chair. One property of luxury
is how quickly we adjust to its inflation.

Hydrangeas huddle, like a city girl's idea
of sheep. A willow drips tallow all over.
Mid-summer. The day lilies make me weep.
None of us knows how soon it will snow.

Over

I walk among wildflowers and trees, chickadees
and cedar waxwings, listening to cicadas' *zzz*'s
and crickets squeaking like the huge, creaky fans
of a factory that dominates some town

out west. Wild grape vines shackle my ankles.
Clouds spackle the sky. I want to cry. I would not
have guessed that a Midwest August could do this.
The thistles' purple tassels still bristle with bees

but the bergamots' tattered lavender
has come apart completely. Chicory's
ultra-violet lights flicker on and off,
as if there were a power shortage.

The meadow's much more yellow now, a flaxen blond,
spring's once-green fields spun into gold.
These new yellows are wool where the pastels
were cotton. The whites look as old

as the faded antimacassars scattered
about our rooms here. Massive mushrooms bloom
in the grass: umbrellas at an outdoor café
where they've served their last glass of iced tea

before Labor Day. Hidden berries fatten
and redden, Christmas ornaments hung out too soon.

Leaves deep in the forest seem to test for rain
like a minister's palms as he urges

his faithful to rise and be saved.
I crave the blue heron's blessing again.
And love. A mourning dove grieves because August is
over. I clutch bald coneflowers' brown balloons,

a circus clown in sepia, waiting
to be carried back to June. But the prairie
keeps changing like a bruise's hues on a woman's face
who's so used to this she no longer makes excuses.

I saw red in one maple I hoped
was a summer tanager, instead of the shock
of that first graying lock on fall's head.
So much of the meadow is already dead.

Prairie clovers' slim stalks burn down like the long
and fragile ash of unflicked cigarettes.
I never picked a single flower this month,
just one of my many regrets.

Maintenon Postcard

Oiseaux with names unknown to me in English too
sing French *chansons* beneath the chestnut trees.
Peonies with ants in them seem American
as I am, transplanted here to this *jardin*
just as accidentally. I wander
in a no-man's-land of language, under
Esperanto skies made more for painters—
who never translate. I want their
freedom, their universal gestures—
like the three brown horses in the chateau's pasture
we saw playing yesterday. . . . I'm at the
Aqueduct Café. To fill the fountains at Versailles
is why they built its local namesake.
But the workers died in droves, sick
with a word I didn't know. Thirsty fleurs-de-lis
decorate their bravery. History
has saved their half-built monument and sacked the kings;
there is *some* justice. And it's breathtaking—
the aqueduct, I mean. (A Roman moon
might mistake this ruin for its own
there's so much time in it; an Egyptian might
recall the sight of Hebrews building pyramids—
it has that height of grandeur and of doom.)
I know that I will dream of it back home.
And now I'd best sign off: I'm out of room.